Contents

Before you read the story

1 What was it like?

a) *Say what you know about your grandparents' lives when they were your age. What was different to your life?*

b) *What's the oldest thing in your house? Describe it in a short text. Then tell the class about it.*

c) *With a partner, talk about what you think life was like a long time ago, e.g. 500 or 1,000 years ago. Think of places in your town or region which could give you ideas: castles, old walls, churches, …*

> I can imagine it was … when my grandparents were young because … |
>
> Back then, people had / didn't have / could / couldn't … |
>
> So it was easier / more difficult / cheaper / more expensive / nicer / … for them. |
>
> I can't imagine how they … because they didn't have …

2 The history of Britain: Important periods

What do you know about life in the past? Match these historical periods with typical things that happened at the time.

1. Celtic Britain (500 BC)
2. Roman Britain (43 AD–410 AD)
3. Norman Britain (1066–1154)
4. The Tudor period (1485–1603)
5. Victorian Britain (1837–1901)

a) Elizabeth I was the Queen of England.
b) People made jewellery with special designs.
c) The Industrial Revolution happened.
d) Poor people sometimes had to make things (e.g. belts) for their lord up in the castle.
e) They built roads, cities and walls in Britain.

1 A day off

"Oh, no! I can't believe it! All that practice for nothing!" said Olivia. She stood outside Thomas Tallis School with Holly, Luke, Jay and Gwen. With sad faces, they were all looking at a big sign: *Sorry – no Sports Day today. Bad weather!* They had looked forward to this Saturday for weeks. But now it was raining hard.

"I think I'll just go home and play video games then," said Jay.

"But we have a whole day free now," Gwen said.

"So come on, let's think of something fun to do!" Luke added.

"I know," said Holly. "Let's go to Greenwich Market. We have to buy a birthday present for Dave – Jay and Luke can give it to him when they go to Cornwall next week."

"Perfect!" Olivia said. "Look – here's a bus now!" And they all got on.

• • •

It was still raining a little when the friends got off the bus. They were walking towards the market and talking about what to buy for Dave. The friends were talking so much that they didn't notice they had turned into a narrow street where they had never been before. It was full of little shops and cafés, but one shop really caught their attention. It had a yellow door and there were colourful lights in the window. A sign above the shop said *Mr Marlow's Emporium*.

The friends stopped and stared at the shop window. It was full of old objects – jewellery, pretty wooden boxes, masks from Africa, a hat with a feather, and lots of colourful plates, bowls, and mugs.

"This is cool!" Holly said in an excited voice.

Jay rolled his eyes and said "It's like a museum – boring!"

"But Dave loves old things!" Olivia said. "Remember that History Club he belongs to?"

"So, let's go in," said Luke, and that's what they did.

A little bell rang as they entered. Inside, it was warm and cosy but it was chaos! There were many more old objects everywhere: a painting of a Spanish dancer, paintings of colourful landscapes, books, games, mirrors, a silver hairbrush, a Victorian calendar with flowers, costumes, and beautiful Elizabethan masks.

"Welcome to my emporium!" said a friendly voice. They all looked around and noticed an older man in a beautiful old chair. "My name is Marlow!" he said. "Please, take your time and look around."

"Thank you, Mr Marlow. We're looking for a present for our friend," said Luke.

"Well, there's something for everyone here!" the friendly man answered. "It's a very special place – you'll see ..."

2 A very Celtic problem

At first, Gwen didn't know what to look at – it was all so special. She walked around for a few minutes and then stopped at a table which was full of beautiful jewellery with Celtic designs – necklaces, bracelets and rings in silver and gold. She noticed a wooden box in the middle of the table that had an interesting silver design.

'Dave likes to collect things,' she thought, 'and he needs somewhere to keep them. Also, a box with a Celtic design would be perfect for a boy in Cornwall.'

"I love this!" she said to Mr Marlow. "How old is it?"

Mr Marlow smiled and said "Oh, this one isn't as old as it looks. But the jewellery is very old! It was made by the Celts – they lived in England from about 500 BC."

Gwen picked up a silver ring and turned it over in her hand. She couldn't stop looking at it and, finally, she just had to put it on.

• • •

"Watch out!" someone called. Gwen turned round and saw two men. They were carrying a pig on a spit. Gwen stared. Where was she? She noticed that she wasn't wearing her glasses. But she could see clearly without them! How could this be? Was this real? Gwen was confused. How had she got there? She had put the ring on in the shop and suddenly she was here. Was she really in the past?

"Who are you?" asked a girl with long, dark hair as she came forward to talk to Gwen. "I haven't seen you before." The girl was wearing a long, brown dress and a belt. "Do you live near here?"

"Er, no," Gwen answered. She realised that she too was wearing a long dress and a belt. It was obvious that Gwen was a stranger, but the girl didn't know that Gwen had come from another century. What could Gwen tell her? She needed a quick answer.

"I live in a village a few miles from here," she then said. "I was helping my brother to find his horse – it often runs away. Anyway, we found the horse, but then my brother rode away as a joke and I got lost in the forest. I walked for hours – and now I'm here."

The girl wasn't at all surprised. "Oh, my brothers and sisters often play tricks on me too. I'm glad you're here! You can tell me all about your village – I've never been outside this one. Oh, and my name is Ula."

"I'm Gwen," Gwen said.

"Today is our 'Summer's End' festival," Ula went on. "That's why everyone is so busy. Oh, this is fun! I've never met anyone new. I hope you don't have to go home straight away. My brothers will help you to find your way later."

Ula pulled Gwen towards a group of wooden houses and barns. She could smell smoke everywhere. The houses were all round and strange-looking. There were small fields all around with animals in them and there was a high fence around the whole village.

"We have to keep wild animals and strangers out," Ula explained. "But not friendly strangers, like you!" she added.

• • •

Ula pulled Gwen into the nearest round house. Inside, it was dark and smoky. There was just one room and no windows. There was a woman at a weaving loom, and a big fire was burning. Gwen could see wool in many different colours all over the floor. She couldn't imagine what it was like to live in a round house like this whose only light was the fire. They didn't have electric lights! How could they see anything?

"Gwen, this is my mother, Nara," Ula said.

"Hello Gwen – are you here to help Ula? She has a lot to do to get ready."

"Get ready? For what?" asked Gwen.

"I'll explain later," whispered Ula.

"Ula, where have you been all day?" asked Nara. She turned to Gwen. "I'm trying to teach Ula the skills she'll need to become a good wife," said Nara. "There's a lot to learn before the wedding – but Ula isn't very interested and she goes out all the time. Girls of my generation did what their mothers told them!"

Wedding? Gwen thought this was very strange. "How old are you, Ula?"

"I don't know," Ula replied. But Gwen guessed that she was no older than fourteen. "Come and meet my father now," Ula said as she took Gwen's hand again.

"You see," said Nara. "She never stays inside and I have so much to teach her. Make sure you girls come back for the feast tonight!"

"What wedding?" Gwen asked as soon as they were outside. Ula stopped smiling for the first time.

"Oh, I'm sure it's the same where you come from?" she said. "I'm a girl, so I have to get married. My brothers can go out to attack other tribes and have adventures and fun, but I have to stay at home and learn how to cook and weave. And then I have to move away from here to take care of my husband's family. Do you think that's fair? I don't! I mean, we girls learn to ride horses and fight with weapons. We grow up to be strong, like our brothers. So, why can't we have some adventures too?"

Gwen didn't know what to say. Was this really an everyday situation for Celtic girls? What a strange lifestyle they had …

"Do you *have to* get married?" she asked in the end. "I mean, can't you just say no?"

"It's difficult," Ula answered. "The boy they have chosen for me is a good person, the chief says. And everyone listens to the chief. So, I will have to marry that boy. Anyway, the whole village is already organising the wedding."

"When is it?" Gwen asked.

"In three days," Ula replied, and then she smiled again. "But maybe I have an idea: I was very lucky to meet you today. Now, let's go and meet my father. He makes jewellery like the ring you're wearing, with beautiful designs."

Ula took Gwen across a field and waved at two boys who were cutting down a tree with big axes. "My brothers," she said.

"Hey Ula!" called one of the boys. "Who's your friend? Does she want to get married too?"

"This is Gwen, and no, she doesn't want to get married!" Ula shouted back. "I see you're back from your battle with the neighbours."

"Oh yes," replied the other brother. "They were so scared of us! They ran away into the forest so we didn't even have to fight."

Next, they entered a hot and smoky barn where Ula's father was making a beautiful gold ring.

"It's for my husband," whispered Ula. "You see, it will be very difficult for me to say no to him now!"

"Ula, you should be at home with your mother," said her father. "She has a lot to teach you before your wedding."

"I see your problem, Ula," said Gwen. "But you said you had an idea … ?"

"Yes. Well, I told you about our Summer's End feast tonight. There will be music and dancing and stories and lots of food. You'll have to taste the roast pig! Anyway, here's my plan: When everyone is having fun, we'll ask my brothers to take you back to your village on their horses … and then I'll go too. I'll just say I want to see where you live. Then, when we arrive, I'll run into the forest. My brothers won't look for me for long – they'll want to get back to the feast. Then, you can come and find me in the forest near your house tomorrow – and I'll stay with you and your family until after my wedding day."

"But …" said Gwen. How could she explain that the plan would never work because she didn't actually live in another village? And how could she get back to her own time?

"Don't worry," said Ula. "I know my family will be worried and angry with me, but I'll go home soon and I think they'll understand. Then at least I'll be free – until they find another husband for me.

"Maybe it'll work," said Gwen, but she felt terrible because she knew she couldn't really help her new friend and she didn't know if she had to stay in the past forever.

When they returned to Ula's house, Ula and Nara decorated Gwen's hair with flowers and they all went together to enjoy the celebration. Gwen couldn't believe the sights, sounds and smells all around her – the meat on the fire, the loud music, the colourful costumes, the stories, the dancing ... she would remember this day forever!

"It's all ready," Ula said. "My brothers are bringing their horses now. They have agreed that I can go too."

"I'll just say goodbye to your mother then." Gwen smiled, but inside she was very worried. How could she tell Ula and her brothers the truth, that she didn't come from here? She started to walk towards Ula's house but it was dark away from the fire. A cat ran in front of her and, as she fell over it, her ring fell off her finger.

3 Victorian dreams

Jay had forgotten all about Sports Day now and was starting to enjoy himself in Mr Marlow's shop. He was looking at some paintings and posters from the Victorian period. One of the posters had the caption *Your world is getting bigger!* He tried to imagine what it was like to travel on one of the first steam trains. How exciting to see the world outside your village for the first time! Life in Britain really changed fast during Queen Victoria's reign, he was sure.

One of the paintings on the wall showed a train carriage full of people. There were big trunks everywhere and no space to move. A boy was looking out of the window – his face was very sad. Jay saw an old Victorian train ticket on a table and picked it up.

• • •

"Can you move over a bit? I can't feel my legs," said a voice. Jay looked around. For a short moment, everything was out of focus. But then he realised that he was in the train carriage from the painting! He was sitting between a girl and the sad boy and nobody could breathe.

"Sorry," Jay said. "I'll try, but ..."

"It doesn't matter," said the boy. "It's an awful day anyway and nothing can make it better."

Jay sat quietly for a moment and tried to enjoy the experience of travelling on a steam train. The seats were wooden and very uncomfortable. And the train moved so slowly! The trains Jay usually went on were much faster. He didn't mind because he liked to look at all the little villages they passed, but the people in the carriage were scared.

"I can't look out! The train is going too fast, we'll crash!" said a woman.

"My poor body!" a man shouted. "This will break my bones!"

Jay was thinking how much more scared these people would be if they could travel in the *really* fast trains of the 21st century.

Jay really wanted to know where the train was going, but these people would think he was crazy if he asked them. Finally, he turned to the boy.

"Excuse me, but I'm not sure if I got on the right train. Where's this one going?" he asked.

"To Liverpool," the boy answered. "I think we're almost there. It'll be the start of my nightmare!"

"Oh good, I'm on the right train!" said Jay. "But what nightmare? – Er, oh, my name is Jay."

"I'm Henry – and I'm going to leave for Australia with my family tonight. But I'd rather stay here alone than go with them. My father lost his factory job in Manchester because the machines now do a lot of his work; the machines are faster. They say the Industrial Revolution is a good thing but I'm not so sure about that. My parents had the crazy idea that we could all move to Australia. Australia! I mean, do you know how far away that is? Over ten thousand miles! The journey will take over three months! I've told them again and again that Australia is where they send prisoners. If they want to give me an education as a criminal, Australia might be a great choice. But I ask them if a life of crime, blood and murder is what they really want for me."

"Good point! I mean, who wants to live with murderers and people like that?" said Jay. "So what do your parents say?"

"They say that Australia isn't just for prisoners any more. More and more people like us go there now because they dream of a better life. Some people even say there's gold there. But I was born in Manchester; I've grown up there and I don't want to leave my friends."

Jay thought about how Dave had moved to Cornwall with his family. Dave hadn't wanted to go at first, but Jay and Luke had already visited him twice and they were going to go again soon. Dave texted with his old friends almost every day – but in the Victorian period there were no smartphones of course. If Henry went to Australia, he would never see or speak to his friends again. How awful! And the ship would be much worse than the train. Jay thought about how he always got sick on boats after only a few minutes. What would three months at sea be like? He wouldn't want to experience that.

"Liverpool Station! Liverpool Station!" a man shouted loudly into the door of the carriage. Everyone pushed their way to the train doors and men helped them get all their heavy trunks off the train.

"Where's your trunk?" asked Henry.

"Oh, I haven't got one," said Jay. "I'm just visiting ... but I'll come with you to the harbour, if you like."

"Sure," said Henry. "Maybe you can persuade my parents to change their minds!" He pointed at a man and a woman in front of them.

Jay and Henry walked behind all the people down towards the harbour. Jay could feel the excitement in the air.

Henry's father turned back and waited for them. "The ship leaves at seven thirty this evening," he said. You two can go and enjoy yourselves for a while but they'll close the gate at six forty-five. Don't be late, Henry! And be careful."

"Great," whispered Henry. "Now I can run away!"

The boys walked away from the harbour and soon found themselves in a small, dark street. Outside one of the little houses there was an old man at a table. He had a big, white beard and he was wearing a blue cap. He was smoking tobacco out of an old clay pipe, telling jokes and talking loudly to everyone as they passed.

"Ahoy there!" he said to Jay and Henry. "Are you boys waiting for that beautiful ship to take you to a new life in Australia? What luck!"

"Luck?" said Henry. "I don't think so. Who knows what our new life will be like? My father says it'll be better than now. But how does he know?"

"Oh, I'd like to be in your shoes!" said the man. "And maybe your father is right ..."

"Are you a sailor?" Jay asked. The man looked exactly like the old sailors he had seen in films.

"Well, I *was* a sailor," he answered. "Sailor Sam, that was me! Of course, I'm a bit too old now – they say I can't sail any more, so I just have to sit here day after day and talk to you young people who have a whole Australian adventure in front of you still!"

Henry walked away and Jay whispered to Sam, "I'm not going to leave for Australia, just Henry. But he doesn't want to go. He says he might run away today. Can you tell him something to make him feel better?"

"Ha! Well, you've come to exactly the right person!" answered Sam. "Actually, I've got some secret information that could change his whole future. I've been waiting for the right person to tell and I think Henry could be the one!"

"Henry, come here and listen to Sam!" Jay shouted.

Henry walked back to the table and Sam took an old piece of paper out of his pocket. The boys stared as he showed them a map and some instructions.

"Look carefully, Henry," said Sam. This is the port in Melbourne, Australia. These instructions will take you to a small hotel. Not many people know about it, but it's a cheap, quiet place for your family to stay for a night or two when you arrive. Ask the owner if you can sleep in Room 2. Under the bed there is a broken floorboard and underneath it, you'll find a black bag. It's full of gold coins – enough for your family to afford a very comfortable life in a new country.

"But ..." said Henry. He couldn't believe what Sailor Sam was saying. "How do I know it's true? And why are you telling *me*?"

"You'll just have to trust me," said Sam. "But it *is* true – there is gold in Australia. I was lucky and, with the help of some friends, I found a lot. But gold coins are heavy and I couldn't bring them all back to England. Anyway, I didn't want the other sailors on the ship to know about them. So I hid them in Room 2 at the hotel and thought I'd bring them back next time – but now there won't be a next time. I'm not allowed to sail again. So, go with your family to Australia and find my gold. I know you'll have a great future!"

'Wow,' Jay thought to himself. He knew that Australia wouldn't be a nightmare for Henry at all if Sam was telling the truth. Jay looked up at a big clock on the wall. "Henry, it's six thirty-five! You've only got ten minutes to get back to the ship! Come on!"

He knew that Henry wasn't thinking about running away any more. There was gold and it was waiting for him under a floorboard in a Melbourne hotel.

"Thank you, Sam!" they shouted as they ran down towards the ship. They could hear the ship's horn – it was ready to leave. Jay waved goodbye to his new friend.

He had no idea how to get home to his own time, so he started to walk back to the station. When he took his ticket out of his pocket, the wind blew it away, and everything was suddenly out of focus again.

4 Drama at the Globe

Olivia was looking at a display of things from the time when Queen Elizabeth I reigned. There was a quill – Olivia felt excited to think that Shakespeare probably used one just like it to write all his famous plays. And there were some beautiful Elizabethan masks. One even had some small jewels on it. Olivia thought about how the Tudor monarchs had such good taste, especially Elizabeth. She had seen a picture of her with a crown. And then Olivia saw some wigs. "These are much better than the ones we use when we do plays at school," she finally said.

"Ah, well, they're original!" Mr Marlow replied. "They came from the Globe Theatre in London, from the early 1600s. And do you know why some of the actors had to wear wigs?"

"Er, no," answered Olivia.

"Well, women and girls weren't allowed to act in theatres back then, so boys had to act as girls!"

"But that isn't fair! Some girls are very good actors!" Olivia answered.

"That's what we think today, but back in the 1600s people didn't think that acting was a suitable job for a girl."

"That's crazy!" Olivia said. She picked up one of the masks and tried it on.

• • •

Olivia found herself on the stage in Shakespeare's Globe Theatre! The theatre didn't have a roof, but the stage had one and it was painted with stars. It was beautiful! Olivia remembered from school that the Globe had burned down in 1613, but it had been rebuilt. 'But what year is it now: before or after the fire?' She had no idea, it was all very confusing.

"One two three, one two three …" a tall man shouted loudly. He was training a group of dancers. And there were musicians playing above, on and underneath the stage.

Olivia didn't know how she had got there. But she noticed that she was still wearing the Elizabethan mask from Mr Marlow's shop, and also a nice, long dress.

The dancers around Olivia were all wearing masks too. Some were wearing men's clothes and some dancers were wearing women's dresses.

But the dancers in women's dresses were all boys! Olivia smiled as she realised what it was like back in the days of Shakespeare.

"Hey, you!" shouted the tall man and looked right at Olivia. She was sure that he was the director of the play.

"Don't just stand there!" he shouted and everybody turned to look at Olivia. This made her feel very nervous. What should she do?

"You aren't trying hard enough!" the director shouted again. "Now, let's try harder this time. Ready? One two three, one two three ..." This time Olivia tried to keep up with the others and she danced with them. It wasn't a difficult dance to learn, but Olivia was confused. Everything was so strange, and she couldn't do the steps very well.

"Where's Thomas?" the director shouted even more loudly than before. Everybody stopped. "We can't play *Romeo and Juliet* without our Juliet!"

"He's got stage fright!" replied the actor who was playing Romeo. "Thomas forgot all his words when we were practising earlier."

The director laughed. "I don't know why he's worried. Everybody knows that the audiences here don't pay much attention to the actors anyway. They shout, eat, drink, walk around, and even fight sometimes. Often, they don't hear a word the actors say. So tell Thomas to come back right now! Otherwise, he'll never work here again!"

"We don't know where he's hiding," said another actor. "We can't find him."

"Well, look more carefully; we don't have time for this! The audience is already waiting outside," the director shouted.

"I can try to find him, if you like," Olivia said.

"Thank you," said the director. "And for the rest of you, back to the masked ball scene."

They started practising their dance again while Olivia opened the stage door.

Outside the theatre, the sun was shining brightly. It was very noisy. Hundreds of excited people were waiting and there was street entertainment. A group of boys were playing bowls and shouting loudly.

'Hmm, I don't think Thomas would walk out of the theatre in his costume,' Olivia thought.

She closed the door and moved back into the shadows behind the stage. It was very dark, but she could just see a boy in a dress sitting on the floor. He wasn't wearing a mask but a wig of long blonde hair. And his hands were full of papers.

Olivia made sure that her mask was still hiding her face – she didn't want the boy to know that she was a girl.

"Thomas?" she asked and the boy looked up at her. "I see that you're having a really bad day."

"Who are you?" asked Thomas. "I don't think I've seen you before."

Olivia didn't know how to explain that she had put on a mask and travelled over 400 years back in time to the golden age of Shakespeare.

"I think I was sent here to help you today," she said. "The director is very worried."

"Well, he doesn't understand what it's like!" said Thomas. "He tells us what to do, but we're the ones who have to remember all the words, in front of over a thousand people. Look at all these lines I have to learn!"

"Well, I understand that you're nervous," Olivia said.

"It's worse than nervous!" Thomas said angrily. "Juliet is my first big role and I feel sick when I think about it. I *can't* act in front of all those people!"

"Why did you decide to be an actor then?" Olivia asked.

"I thought it would be fun – and I needed some money," said Thomas. "My family didn't like the idea, of course. Nobody thinks that acting is a good job. Maybe they were right."

"Listen, Thomas," said Olivia. "Without a Juliet, the director will have to cancel the play, the other actors won't get any money, and all the audience will have to go home. You think you feel bad now, but you'll feel much worse if that happens!"

Olivia could see that Thomas was listening to her. "Anyway," she said, as she remembered what the director had said about the audience, "all the people are here for a fun day out. They'll be so noisy that they won't notice if you forget a few words. Go on – after the first time, it'll be much easier. Things always come most easily after you've done them a few times. And William Shakespeare is such a great writer. It'll be fun!"

"Well – I'll try," Thomas said slowly. Olivia smiled happily. 'All's well that ends well!' she thought. She took his hand, and together they stepped out of the shadows.

"There you are!" shouted the director as he saw Thomas. "Thank you, you've saved my life!" he said to Olivia.

Just then, a door opened and hundreds of people hurried inside the theatre. They were laughing, shouting and pushing each other.

From behind the stage, Olivia and Thomas watched the beginning of the play. Lots of other actors went onto the stage first. But finally, it was Thomas's turn. An actor dressed up as a nurse called "Where's that girl? Juliet!"

Thomas entered the stage confidently and said in a loud, clear voice "Who calls?"

"Your mother," replied the nurse.

Olivia was really enjoying the play. Nobody was paying any attention to her, so she wanted to take off her mask to be able to see better. But as she took it off, Thomas's voice suddenly became quieter and quieter.

5 I want to go home!

At the shop, Luke had found a table full of strange old games.

"Did people really play with these?" he asked.

"Of course," said Mr Marlow. "They're Roman, and very old; probably from 50 or 100 AD."

Luke looked more closely at the objects on the table. There was something that looked like a dice game. The dice were made of bone and, suddenly, he really wanted to touch them – but not in front of Mr Marlow. Two thousand years old! He needed to be very careful. When Mr Marlow finally turned away, Luke picked up one of the dice and rolled it carefully onto the table.

• • •

"Ha! You got four. That means I win!" said a voice. Luke stared. He was sitting at a stone table in the middle of a village, and in front of him was a young man who was wearing a tunic, a belt and sandals. And Luke was wearing similar clothes.

"Good!" the young man said. "That's two games each – we'll have to play again to decide the winner."

Luke couldn't speak – he was too surprised. He felt as if he was dreaming. He looked around and saw other young men who were sitting at tables around the square and also playing dice games. The square was noisy and busy. There were buildings all around it – houses, shops and public baths – and there were people everywhere. Children were running across the square, playing ball games, and dogs were chasing them. Luke looked up and saw that there was a high wall around the whole town. In the distance, he could see another wall. It was very long and he couldn't see the end of it because it disappeared into the countryside and the clouds.

"Hey, Marius! We have to get back to the barracks now," someone called to the young man who was playing dice with Luke.

"Come with us, Lucius!" said Marius to Luke. "You've always wanted to see what our life is like up on Hadrian's Wall. There are hundreds of soldiers like us there – nobody will notice you if you stay close to us."

"… and you can help us to carry all the food and supplies back," said one of the others. "At least we'll eat well tonight."

'So, they call me Lucius,' Luke thought to himself as he put the dice back in his pocket. 'Not a bad Roman name.' He had travelled back to Roman times – and he was excited.

All the young soldiers knew Luke (Lucius). He listened carefully to their conversations while they were walking up towards the long wall he had seen from the square. He learned that they lived in the barracks on a part of the wall near the town. Every day some of them came down into town to collect food and supplies. And sometimes, they had a bath in the public bath house.

"I love to have a bath every few weeks, even if I don't need it," said Marius.

In this way, the soldiers had met people from the town. They enjoyed having fun with Lucius and his friends because their life on the wall was so hard. They had come from Rome and the emperor Hadrian had sent them and thousands of other young soldiers to invade England and to found new towns there. Their job had been to build a wall across the north of England to fight Scottish tribes like the Picts and to keep them out of the Roman Empire. Marius was sad when he talked about his home in Rome, and Luke had a lot of questions for him.

Soon, they all arrived at a big gate and two guards watched as all the soldiers went through. Luke was nervous for a moment but stayed with the group. As Marius had said, nobody noticed him. They left all the supplies in a big storehouse. Then Luke followed Marius into his barracks.

"Oh, you haven't got much space!" said Luke. The room was bare, with four beds on each side and – nothing else.

"You're right," Marius replied. "Eight of us sleep here – and it's cold and uncomfortable. Not like the nice houses we Romans have built in your town. You people are lucky we came here. Your homes are so much better than before – and now you have clean water, underfloor heating and good roads. But, I'm sorry we can't do anything about the awful weather!"

"What was your life like in Rome?" asked Luke.

"I lived with my family in a big, beautiful house," Marius answered sadly. "My father is a very important man there. We had glass windows, mosaic floors and wall paintings – nothing like my bedroom at the barracks here. I went to school and there were always exciting events in town, like chariot races."

"Did you *have to* come to England?" asked Luke. He couldn't imagine leaving such a nice life.

"No," answered Marius. "But I did something stupid. Some of my older friends joined the army and they were excited to go to England. They laughed at me because I had to stay in Rome; they said my life was boring. But I wanted an adventure too, so I ran away from home and joined the army. I had to lie about my age – I'm only fifteen. You have to be seventeen to be a soldier."

'So that's why Marius was sad when he talked about his life back in Rome,' thought Luke.

"I really want to go home," Marius continued, "but if I ask my commander, I'll have to tell him that I lied about my age and then I'll really be in trouble. My only hope is that he knew my father in Rome and might decide to help me, as a favour to my family. But he's often in a bad mood – and he could make my life very difficult if he wanted to."

Luke felt bad for his friend. He really wanted to make him feel better. But, just at that moment, the door opened noisily and an older soldier shouted "Outside! Now! Time for your training!"

"That's our commander," explained Marius. "He's in a bad mood today! Now, come outside with us and hide in those big trees over there." He pointed out of the window. "You'll see what our life here is really like."

Luke ran out of the barracks and quickly hid among the trees. The soldiers had to run, jump and pretend to fight each other with heavy wooden weapons while the commander shouted at them. Next, the commander told them to put their heavy backpacks on. He didn't care that some of the boys and men had bloody hands and feet from all the hard work and training.

"You know the rules!" he shouted. "You have the whole afternoon to march twenty miles, until sunset. No resting, keep moving! Tomorrow we're going to fight the Picts and I need you all to train hard and be strong, fit and ready to win the battle! Maybe we can even capture some of those Picts and sell them as slaves. Now, go!"

Marius and his group marched close to the trees where Luke was hiding and Marius was able to whisper to Luke.

"When I'm back, we can have another dice game. But please think about my problem while I'm away. I've had enough of my adventure!"

Luke couldn't imagine how tired and hungry Marius and the others would be when they returned. This was no life for a fifteen-year-old boy whose family and friends were so far away. Maybe the commander would feel sorry for Marius when he found out his real age. Maybe Marius wasn't the only one – a lot of boys wanted to have adventures.

Luke was having an adventure right now – and he loved it, although he was a bit worried that he would have to stay in Roman times forever. In his time, he didn't have to train in the mud and dirt every day or live in the cold, uncomfortable barracks.

Luke sat and thought about what to do until it was nearly dark. Deep in thought, he took the dice out of his pocket and rolled it from one hand to the other. Suddenly, he dropped the dice and it landed on the ground.

6 I didn't do it!

Holly was surprised that her friends were so silent while they were in Mr Marlow's shop. They usually talked and joked and argued all the time. But today, everyone was in their own separate world.

She opened a wardrobe in a corner and found that it was full of long, colourful dresses. They reminded her of old films about the Middle Ages, like in Norman times. Then she noticed a dark green cloak. She took it out of the cupboard, put it on carefully, and looked at herself in the mirror.

• • •

"Are you going up to the castle to see your friend Matilda again?" said a voice Holly didn't know. "You worked hard this morning. The house is very clean. So go and enjoy yourself for an hour or two, daughter dear!"

Holly looked more closely into the mirror and, behind her, she saw a woman who was wearing a long, blue dress. This was her *mother*? She turned around. She was in a small, cosy room with a fire. Through a small window, she could see that the snow was falling hard.

"Oh, and Holly, can you stop at the market on your way back and bring me some vegetables?" asked the woman. "But that cloak you're wearing is too thin – it's cold outside! Here, take it off and wear mine." She put her much thicker, grey cloak around Holly's shoulders. "And put your boots on too," she added.

"Here's some money for the vegetables," said the woman and gave Holly some coins. "Go quickly now, before the snow gets worse."

"All right. Bye!" said Holly. How could she explain that she didn't know how to find the castle or the market? She closed the door behind her and hoped she would find them easily.

• • •

Holly walked into the small village and saw a castle up on the hill in front of her. It looked like something she had seen in one of her history books, from the days of William the Conqueror. She was excited to meet her new friend, Matilda. Now she just had to find her!

When she was nearly at the castle gate, a girl ran out to meet her.

"Holly, come quickly," the girl said. "Matilda needs your help!"

'They know my name here? How strange!' Holly thought to herself.

"Why? What happened?" Holly answered.

"It's awful," said the girl. "Someone has stolen a silver necklace from Lady Beatrice. Her ladyship says that Matilda took it – but she didn't! I know she wouldn't do anything like that!"

"Where is Matilda?" asked Holly.

"She's hiding in the kitchen with the kitchen maids," said the girl. "Lady Beatrice is angry and doesn't want Matilda to be her lady-in-waiting any more. Matilda is very upset."

"I don't know how I can help," said Holly.

"Just come and talk to her. You're her best friend and she'll feel better if she sees you," said the girl.

The two girls walked up to the castle. The gardens were white with snow and people in fine clothes were walking along and speaking French to each other.

Holly couldn't understand them very well. She thought about how she needed to work harder on her French back at TTS.

She looked into the windows of the castle and saw beautiful rooms with big colourful tapestries on the walls, thick carpets and big fires. It was a wonderful life in the castle, she was sure.

Finally, they arrived at the kitchen. A girl was crying and four kitchen maids were trying to make her feel better.

"Holly! It's so awful," cried Matilda. "Her ladyship is thinking about what my future here at the castle will be, but I don't *have* a future here if she really believes that I stole her necklace."

"What do you think happened to it?" asked Holly.

"I don't know!" answered Matilda. "Her ladyship keeps all her jewellery in a cupboard in her room. But a lot of people work here at the castle – it would be easy for someone to get in and take things."

"What would you do if you had to leave the castle?" Holly asked.

"It would be terrible!" Matilda replied. "Working for the Beauchamp family is perfect for a girl like me. And lady-in-waiting is the best position! You know how hard I worked to become a lady-in-waiting," Matilda added. "My parents are so proud that I work here. You know they live a long way from here so I can't see them very often. But I'm so happy that I can send them money, and they're happy that I have – or had – a good life."

"Please don't worry," said Holly. "*We* know you didn't steal anything. Now, I have to go to the market for my mother, but I'll think about what you can do."

"Come back soon!" said Matilda. "I can't hide here in the kitchen all day!"

Holly walked back down the hill towards the market. It was very noisy and colourful and everyone wanted to stop and talk to her. She found a man who was selling vegetables and bought a large bag to take home. Then, she noticed a girl who was standing behind a table full of scarves, belts, and jewellery. It was the most colourful of all the market stalls.

"Come and look!" said the girl, and Holly walked over to look more closely. She picked up a belt.

"Did you make this yourself?" Holly asked.

"Yes," said the girl, "I'm Linn. I make lots of belts like this, but I have to give most of them to the lord at the castle for his men. And my mother and sister make lots of these scarves, but they have to give them to the ladies at the castle. And my father and brother work every day on the land to grow the vegetables that you just bought. But they have to give most of them to the family at the castle. It's terrible: We work so hard and have to give nearly everything to those rich Normans."

"But that isn't fair!" said Holly.

"I know!" Linn answered. "So, I keep a few things like these and try to make a little money where I can."

"Surely you don't make the jewellery too?" said Holly.

"Er, no," said Linn, a bit embarrassed.

Holly picked up a silver necklace. She turned it over in her hand and noticed the letters 'B.B.' on the back. "Where did you get this from?" she asked.

"My friend brings me jewellery sometimes," Linn answered. "I don't know where he gets it from but people love it and pay me good money for it. Would you like to buy it?"

Holly thought quickly. She felt like a detective. "Listen," she said. "I think this necklace came from the castle. I don't know how your friend got it, but my friend, Matilda, is in big trouble. She is Lady Beatrice Beauchamp's lady-in-waiting, and Lady Beatrice thinks that Matilda stole a silver necklace from her. Matilda is going to lose her job and her family is very poor. I must take this necklace back to the castle."

Linn was quiet for a moment. Finally she said, "My family is very poor too."

"Please think about it!" Holly said. "I'll take these vegetables to my mother, and then I'll come back here. We can go to the castle together and ask to speak to Lady Beatrice. You know it's the right thing to do."

Linn looked very worried. If she went to the castle, Lady Beatrice would ask her how she had got the necklace – and she didn't want her friend to get into trouble too.

"All right, I'll think about it," Linn answered. "I'll tell you my decision when you come back."

Holly ran back to the house, where her 'mother' was waiting for her.

"You took a long time," she said.

"Sorry," said Holly. "Matilda has got a problem ..."

Her 'mother's' thick cloak was wet with snow. Holly took it off and put it by the fire. But she was still cold so she looked for the green cloak she had worn when she arrived and put it around her shoulders.

7 A present for Dave

Holly needed to sit down. Her head was spinning and she felt very tired. Something very strange had just happened to her, but *how* had it happened? It was a mystery. She noticed that the others were sitting on some chairs in the opposite corner of the shop and she went to join them. Nobody was speaking.

Mr Marlow walked over to the friends and sat down with them.

"So, have you enjoyed yourselves in my little emporium?" he asked. "You're all very quiet! How are you feeling?"

"Er – a bit tired," Luke answered.

"Quite strange," said Gwen.

"Confused," was Jay's reply. He felt as if he had just woken up after a long sleep.

Everyone was quiet again. They were all thinking about the places they had just visited. But nobody wanted to talk about it because they were worried that the others wouldn't believe them.

"What about your friend's present?" Mr Marlow asked.

"Present? – Oh, yes. Er, er, I can't think about that right now," Holly answered in a confused voice.

Luke tried hard to focus. "I, er, think we should buy him a game," he said.

"Or a mask," said Olivia.

"Maybe a poster?" Jay suggested.

"We'll never agree!" said Luke. "Anyway, I'm hungry now. Let's go and eat something while we decide. Then we can come back and buy something."

"But why don't you buy something *before* you go?" said Mr Marlow. "Sometimes it's better not to wait."

"You don't know us very well," said Gwen. "We never decide quickly."

"Well, if you really think you need time, you should go and talk about it," Mr Marlow said sadly. "Thank you again for coming to visit me ..."

• • •

Half an hour later, the friends were sitting in small café in the next street. They continued their discussion while they were eating. In the end they agreed that the Celtic box that Gwen had seen was the best idea. They were ready to go back and buy it.

As they were paying for their food, the rain stopped and the sun started shining. Now everyone was in a good mood again and they felt less tired and confused. They still weren't ready to talk to each other about their adventures, but they all knew that they had had an amazing morning. And they had finally agreed on a cool present for Dave!

They walked down the road together and turned the corner into the little road where they had been that morning. They looked all around them for the yellow door, the colourful lights and shop sign but couldn't see it anywhere.

"That's strange," said Luke. "I'm sure it was right here."

"It was," Holly agreed.

But Mr Marlow's Emporium had disappeared and there was nothing left to show that it had ever been there.

8 Epilogue

The friends all agreed that Mr Marlow's Emporium had been a very strange place. How could it have disappeared? As they walked back towards Greenwich Market, the friends were ready to tell each other what had happened to them inside the shop. Olivia spoke first.

"You won't believe this," she said. "I was just trying on an Elizabethan mask and I found myself back in the early 1600s – in the Globe Theatre!" She told her story. "I can't stop thinking about Thomas," she said.

"Well, if I had been Thomas, I would have been scared too!" said Gwen.

"Yes," said Holly. "But he probably gave a great performance in the end. And if he hadn't met Olivia, he couldn't have done it," she added.

Luke was next. "I rolled a Roman dice and the next moment I was in a Roman town near Hadrian's Wall!" he said.

He told the others all about Marius's problem. "I felt really bad for him," he said. "I would love to know if Marius told the commander about his lie. I really hope Marius got back to Rome safely."

"If I had been the commander, I would have felt sorry for him and let him go!" said Jay. "A lot of people want to have adventures and everyone makes mistakes."

Next, it was Gwen's turn. "I put a Celtic ring on my finger and I found myself in a Celtic village!" she said. She told them all about Ula's problem. Nobody could believe it.

"Married!" said Holly. "At fourteen? No!"

"If my parents had found a husband for me at that age, I would have run away too!" said Olivia.

"But if she had run away, she would have missed her family too much," said Gwen. She really wanted to know if Ula's wedding had happened and if she had had a happy life.

Jay was ready to tell his story now. "You know those Victorian paintings I was looking at?" he asked. "Well, I found myself *inside* one of them. I went by steam train to Liverpool!"

He told Henry's story, about how he hadn't wanted to go to Australia and about Sailor Sam's gold coins.

"I hope he was able to find the hotel and find the gold," he said.

"If I had met Sailor Sam, I wouldn't have believed him!" said Luke. "Gold under the floorboards! *Really*?"

"But you didn't meet Sailor Sam," said Jay. "He was very cool and I know he wanted to help Henry. I believed him – I would just like to know that Henry and his family arrived safely in Australia and that he found the gold."

Finally it was Holly's turn, and she told the others about the beautiful Norman castle and about Matilda and Linn.

"I really hope Linn did the right thing and gave the necklace back to Lady Beatrice, so Matilda could keep her job," she said.

"If I had been Linn, I would have gone to the castle and spoken to Lady Beatrice," Gwen said. "It wouldn't have been fair if Matilda had lost her job!"

"But Linn's family were poor too," said Jay. "I don't think she said anything!"

• • •

The discussion continued for a while. Nobody would ever know the answers to all their questions. But two things were sure. They were very happy that they had decided to go into Mr Marlow's Emporium that morning. And now they would have to find another present for Dave.

Exercises

1 Mr Marlow's shop (Part 1)

a) *Are the sentences below right or wrong?*

	right	wrong
1. Olivia, Holly, Luke, Jay and Gwen are happy that there's no Sports Day because of bad weather.		
2. The friends know what they want to buy for Dave.		
3. The friends often go to the narrow street by the market.		
4. Jay isn't interested in Mr Marlow's shop.		
5. Olivia thinks they'll find a good present in the shop.		
6. The shop is very tidy.		

b) *Correct the sentences that are wrong.*

2 Who did what in Celtic times? (Part 2)

Read part 2. Who did these things in Celtic times?	boys/ men	girls/ women	both
1. took part in festivals			
2. attacked other tribes			
3. learned to fight with weapons			
4. often moved to a new village after their wedding			
5. cut down trees with big axes			
6. learned to ride horses			
7. had adventures			
8. wore jewellery			
9. learned to cook and weave			
10. grew up to be strong			

3 Life in Celtic times (Part 2)

a) *Fill in the gaps in the sentences with one word each. The first letter of each word can help you.*

The Celts lived in England about 500 BC. They were famous for their jewellery, like r_______________ **(1)** and n_______________ **(2)**. They made their jewellery from s_______________ **(3)** and g_______________ **(4)** and it had beautiful d_______________ **(5)**. The Celts lived in t_______________ **(6)** and there were often big b_______________ **(7)**, when the men a_______________ **(8)** their neighbours. The women had to take c_______________ **(9)** of their h_______________ **(10)** families and teach the next g_______________ **(11)** of girls how to be good wives. They had no e_______________ **(12)** lights, so they had to make big f_______________ **(13)**, and that was a lot of work. Life wasn't easy back then!

b) *Read page 9, lines 23–29 again. Do you agree with Ula that life isn't fair for the girls? Discuss this with a partner and give reasons for your opinion.*

4 Imagine ... (Part 3)

Read page 12 again and discuss the questions.

a) *How do you think people felt in the 1800s when they travelled by train for the first time? What do you think they found strange, surprising, exciting or maybe scary?*

b) *Tell the others in your group about a time when you travelled to a new city or to another country for the first time. Did you find anything strange, surprising, exciting or scary?*

5 A short summary (Part 3)

Use the words from the box to fill in the gaps in this short summary of part 3.

What luck | comfortable | picks up | experience | secret | seat | is like | Industrial Revolution | factories | turn back | grown up | change their minds | blood and murder | afford

When Jay **(1)** an old train ticket, he suddenly finds himself on a Victorian steam train and meets Henry, who is in the **(2)** next to him. Henry is very upset because he has to go to Australia with his family. His dad lost his job because the **(3)** had brought machines to the **(4)**, so they didn't need so many people to work there. Henry doesn't really know what Australia **(5)**. He has only heard about all the criminals there and stories of **(6)**. He doesn't want that kind of **(7)**! He just wants to **(8)** and go home. Henry has **(9)** in Manchester and he wants to stay there. He wants his parents to **(10)** and Jay doesn't know how to help him. Later that day, they meet a sailor called Sam. Sam tells them his big **(11)** – there's gold under a bed in a hotel in Melbourne. If Henry finds it, his family could **(12)** a very **(13)** life. **(14)**!

6 Back in Tudor times at the Globe Theatre (Part 4)

Match the sentence parts.

1. Boys wore wigs c 2. Olivia felt nervous g 3. Thomas was hiding a 4. The people outside were very noisy d 5. Thomas was scared 6. The audience didn't care if actors forgot their words 7. The director was very happy with Olivia b	because	a) he didn't want to act. b) she helped Thomas to calm down. c) girls couldn't be actors. d) they were excited about the play. e) they just wanted a fun day out. f) Juliet was his first big role. g) the director shouted at her.

7 Good advice? (Part 4)

On page 20, Olivia gives Thomas some advice. She tries in two different ways. Which way do you think works better? Give reasons.

1. "Without a Juliet, the director will have to cancel the play, the other actors won't get any money and all the audience will have to go home. You think you feel bad now, but you'll feel much worse if that happens!"
2. "All the people are here for a fun day out. They'll be so noisy that they won't notice if you forget a few words. After the first time, it'll be much easier. William Shakespeare is such a great writer! It'll be fun!"

8 Marius and Luke (Part 5)

What happens when? Put the events in the correct order. Number them 1 to 10.

☐ A The commander shouts at the soldiers.

☐ B The soldiers travel from Rome to England.

☐ C Marius lives in a beautiful house.

☐ D Marius meets Luke and they play a dice game.

☐ E Marius goes out to fight the Picts.

☐ F Marius invites Luke to visit his barracks.

☐ G Luke thinks about how he could help Marius.

☐ H Marius joins the army.

☐ I The soldiers improve English houses and roads.

☐ J Marius's older friends join the army.

9 Romans in England (Part 5)

Write the missing words in the puzzle below and find the words in the dark boxes.

1. Roman soldiers lived in **(1)**, not in houses.
2. The Romans **(2)** a lot of new towns in England.
3. Hadrian was an important Roman **(3)**.
4. The Romans washed themselves in public **(4)**.
5. On their feet, the Romans wore **(5)**.
6. Soldiers use these when they fight. **(6)**
7. "Don't talk to the commander. He's in a very bad **(7)**!"
8. "Go and **(8)** some Picts and bring them back with you!"
9. The Romans **(9)** England in 43 AD.
10. Roman soldiers had to train in the mud and **(10)**.
11. Underfloor **(11)** was a very good Roman invention.

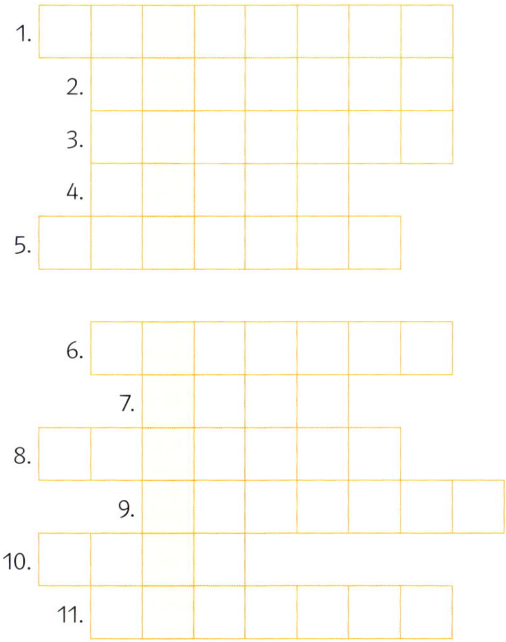

Solution:

10 Your opinion (Part 5)

Can you understand why Marius lied about his age? Give reasons.

11 Who thinks what? (Part 6)

Read part 6. Then read the different thoughts below. Which character do you think they match the best: Holly, Lady Beatrice, Matilda or Linn?

1. I would *never* do that!
2. How will I find the castle and the market?
3. I can't believe she did this. She was my best maid!
4. Wow! What a cool place to live.
5. How can I tell my family? They'll be so angry!
6. I hope that girl buys something from me.
7. Somebody stole this from Lady Beatrice.
8. What about *my* family?
9. It isn't easy to find good maids. Now what will I do?
10. I must persuade her to come to the castle with me!

12 Strange words (Part 6)

Some of the words in the sentences below are very strange. Put the letters in the correct order. The underlined letters should come first.

1. I like films in which a **TEDEVECTI** tries to solve a crime.
2. My neighbour has two sons and a **GADRUTEH**.
3. It often **SWOSN** here in winter and I have to wear my **TOSBO** when I go outside.
4. My grandfather **ROSGW** a lot of vegetables in his garden.
5. I **EWKO PU** really late this morning and missed my bus to school.
6. The **RDLO** and **YDLA** of a Norman castle had a very nice life.

13 To tell or not to tell? (Part 6)

a) *What would you do in Linn's situation: Should she go to the castle and give the necklace back to Lady Beatrice or not? Form two groups. One group collects ideas for why Linn should give back the necklace, the other collects ideas for why she shouldn't.*

b) *Exchange your ideas in class.*

14 Understanding the ending (Part 7)

a) *Answer these questions:*

1. After the friends wake up from their adventures, they feel very strange. What do you think happened to them? Exchange your ideas in class.
2. The friends don't buy a present for Dave before they leave the shop. Why not? What do they do instead?
3. Describe what happens when the friends go back to buy Dave's present.

b) *On page 29, in lines 26–27, Mr Marlow says: "But why don't you buy something before you go? Sometimes it's better not to wait." Why does Mr Marlow say this? Explain why these lines are so important for the whole story.*

c) *Creative writing: Go back to the picture of Mr Marlow's Emporium on p. 6. Look at the different objects. Think of different 'time travel' adventures you could go on if you touched one of those objects. Then write a short text (8–10 lines) about one of those adventures.*

15 Five adventures, five problems (Part 8)

a) *Choose from these writing tasks:*

1. Write a dialogue between Ula and the village chief about the boy he wants her to marry.
2. Henry has arrived in Australia and writes to his cousin in England.
3. Thomas writes to his parents about his first big role at the Globe.
4. Marius decides to tell his commander that he has lied. Write their conversation.
5. Matilda writes to her parents about what has happened at the castle.

b) *Which historical character from the story do you think experiences the most difficult problem? Why?*

Vocabulary

pl.	plural
Norman	Vokabeln aus GL 3 (Bundesausgabe), Unit 3 bzw. GL 3 G9, Unit 4 und GL 3 BW, Unit 3
*Elizabeth I	Vokabeln aus Green Line 3 Baden-Württemberg, Unit 3
sign	neue Vokabeln, die bis GL 3 (Bundesausgabe), Unit 3 bzw. GL 3 G9, Unit 4 und GL3 BW, Unit 3 nicht vorkommen

Before you read the story

Page 4

Norman ['nɔ:mən] Normanne; normannisch
Tudor ['tju:də] Tudor-
Victorian [vɪk'tɔ:riən] viktorianisch; Viktorianer/-in
*Elizabeth I [ɪ,lɪzəbəθ ðə 'fɜ:st] *Königin von England (geboren 1533, regiert ab 1558, gestorben 1603)*
Industrial Revolution [ɪn,dʌstriəl revl'u:ʃn] die industrielle Revolution

Part 1

Page 5

sign [saɪn] Schild
emporium [em'pɔ:riəm] Kaufhaus
object ['ɒbdʒɪkt] Gegenstand
Africa ['æfrɪkə] Afrika
feather ['feðə] Feder
to roll one's eyes [,rəʊl wʌnz‿'aɪz] die Augen verdrehen
cosy ['kəʊzi] gemütlich
chaos ['keɪɒs] Chaos; Durcheinander
Spanish ['spænɪʃ] spanisch
hairbrush ['heəbrʌʃ] Haarbürste
calendar ['kæləndə] Kalender
*Elizabethan [ɪ,lɪzə'bi:θn] Elisabethaner/-in; elisabethanisch

Part 2

Page 7

special ['speʃl] besonders
*which [wɪtʃ] der; die; das; dem; den *(Relativpronomen)*
*design [dɪ'zaɪn] Design; Gestaltung
necklace ['nekləs] Halskette
ring [rɪŋ] Ring
gold [gəʊld] Gold
*that [ðæt] der; die; das; dem; den *(Relativpronomen)*
Celt [kelt] Kelte/Keltin
BC (= before Christ) [,bi:'si:] vor Christus
to pick up [,pɪk‿'ʌp] aufheben
spit [spɪt] *hier:* Bratspieß
forward ['fɔ:wəd] vorwärts; nach vorne
dress [dres] Kleid
belt [belt] Gürtel
*obvious ['ɒbviəs] offensichtlich
stranger ['streɪndʒə] Fremder
to **ride** [raɪd] reiten

Page 8

barn [bɑ:n] Scheune
*to smell [smel] riechen; duften
fence [fens] Zaun
smoky ['sməʊki] verraucht
weaving loom ['wi:vɪŋ ,lu:m] Webstuhl
*to burn [bɜ:n] brennen; verbrennen
wool [wʊl] Wolle

Page 9

what it was like [,wɒt ɪt wɒz 'laɪk] wie es war
*whose [hu:z] dessen *(Relativpronomen)*; deren *(Relativpronomen)*
electric [ɪ'lektrɪk] elektrisch
generation [,ßenE'reɪʃn] Generation
feast [fi:st] Festmahl
tonight [tə'naɪt] heute Abend; heute Nacht
to attack [ə'tæk] angreifen
tribe [traɪb] Stamm; Volksstamm
to take care of sb [,teɪk‿'keər‿əv] sich um jdn. kümmern; für jdn. sorgen

*husband ['hʌzbənd] Ehemann
weapon ['wepən] Waffe
to grow up [ˌgrəʊ_'ʌp] aufwachsen; erwachsen werden
everyday ['evrideɪ] alltäglich
lifestyle ['laɪfstaɪl] Lebensstil; Lifestyle
to marry ['mæri] heiraten

Page 10

to **wave** [weɪv] winken
*who [hu:] der; die; das; dem; den *(Relativpronomen)*
axe [æks] Axt
battle ['bætl] Schlacht; Kampf
to **say no** [seɪ 'nəʊ] Nein sagen
to taste [teɪst] schmecken; probieren
to **run** [rʌn] laufen

Page 11

*terrible ['terəbl] schrecklich; schlimm; furchtbar

Part 3

Page 12

*caption ['kæptʃə] Bildunterschrift
reign [reɪn] Herrschaft
carriage ['kærɪdʒ] Kutsche
trunk [trʌŋk] Truhe
out of focus [ˌaʊt_əv 'fəʊkəs] unscharf
*seat [si:t] Sitz; Sitzplatz
uncomfortable [ʌn'kʌmftəbl] unbequem
crash [kræʃ] zusammenstoßen
bone [bəʊn] Knochen
start [stɑ:t] Anfang; Start
nightmare ['naɪtmeə] Albtraum

Page 13

*I'd rather [aɪd 'rɑ:ðə] Ich würde lieber
factory ['fæktri] Fabrik; Werk
prisoner ['prɪzənə] Gefangene/-r; Sträfling
education *(no pl.)* [ˌedʒʊ'keɪʃn] Erziehung; Bildung
blood [blʌd] Blut
murder ['mɜ:də] Mord

point [pɔɪnt] *hier:* Argument
*murderer ['mɜ:drə] Mörder/-in
to be born [bi 'bɔ:n] geboren werden

Page 14

to **text** [tekst] eine SMS schreiben
to experience [ɪk'spɪəriəns] erfahren; erleben
harbour ['hɑ:bə] Hafen
to change one's mind [ˌtʃeɪndʒ wʌnz 'maɪnd] seine Meinung ändern
*to turn back [ˌtɜ:n 'bæk] umkehren; zurückgehen
themselves [ðəm'selvz] sich
beard [bɪəd] Bart
cap [kæp] Kappe
tobacco *(no pl.)* [tə'bækəʊ] Tabak
*to pass [pɑ:s] durchgehen; vorbeigehen (an)
Ahoy there! [ə'hɔɪ ˌðeə] Ahoi, ihr beiden!
What luck! [ˌwɒt 'lʌk] Was für ein Glück!

Page 15

secret ['si:kət] geheim

Page 16

owner ['əʊnə] Besitzer(in)
floorboard ['flɔ:bɔ:d] Dielenbrett
to afford [ə'fɔ:d] sich leisten
*comfortable ['kʌmftəbl] bequem; komfortabel

Part 4

Page 17

*to display [dɪ'spleɪ] anzeigen
to reign [reɪn] herrschen; regieren
*quill [kwɪl] Federkiel
jewel ['dʒu:əl] Juwel; Edelstein
monarch ['mɒnək] Monarch
*crown [kraʊn] Krone
wig [wɪg] Perücke
play [pleɪ] Theaterstück
the Globe Theatre [ðə ˌgləʊb 'θɪətə] *Theater in London*

*back then [bæk 'ðen] damals
suitable ['su:təbl] passend; angemessen
stage [steɪdʒ] Bühne
*to burn down [ˌbɜ:n 'daʊn] abbrennen; niederbrennen
*to rebuild [ˌri:'bɪld] wieder aufbauen

Page 18

*right [raɪt] *hier:* direkt

Page 19

stage fright ['steɪdʒ ˌfraɪt] Lampenfieber
*audience ['ɔ:diəns] Publikum
*otherwise ['ʌðəwaɪz] sonst
masked ball [ˌmɑ:skt 'bɔ:l] Maskenball
bright [braɪt] hell
noisy ['nɔɪzi] laut
entertainment *(no pl.)* [ˌentə'teɪnmənt] Unterhaltung
*to play bowls [ˌpleɪ 'bəʊlz] Bowling spielen
shadow ['ʃædəʊ] Schatten
golden age [ˌgəʊldn 'eɪdʒ] goldenes Zeitalter

Page 20

to **cancel sth** ['kænsl] etw. absagen
worse [wɜ:s] schlechter
William Shakespeare [ˌwɪljəm 'ʃeɪkspɪə] *englischer Dramatiker (1564–1616)*
writer ['raɪtə] Autor/-in; Verfasser/-in
*All's well that ends well. [ˌɔ:lz wel ðət 'ndz wel] Ende gut, alles gut.
to **step** [step] treten

Part 5

Page 21

AD (= Anno Domini) [ˌeɪ'di:] nach Christus
to **touch** [tʌtʃ] berühren
careful ['keəfl] vorsichtig
tunic ['tju:nɪk] Kittel
cloak [kləʊk] Umhang
sandal ['sændl] Sandale
as if [əz‿'ɪf] als ob
square [skweə] Platz

baths *(pl.)* [bɑ:θs] Badehaus; Therme
to **disappear** [ˌdɪsə'pɪə] verschwinden
barrack ['bærək] Kaserne
Lucius [lu:ʃəs] *römischer Name*
supplies *(pl.)* [sə'plaɪz] Lieferung

Page 22

emperor ['emprə] Kaiser
to invade [ɪn'veɪd] einmarschieren (in); eindringen (in); überfallen
to found [faʊnd] gründen
Pict [pɪkt] Pikte/Piktin
Roman Empire [ˌrəʊmən 'empaɪə] Römisches Reich

Page 23

gate [geɪt] Tor
storehouse ['stɔ:haʊs] Kaufhaus
underfloor heating [ˌʌndəflɔ: 'hi:tɪŋ] Fußbodenheizung
mosaic [məʊ'zeɪɪk] Mosaik
chariot race ['tʃæriət ˌreɪs] Streitwagen-Rennen
commander [kə'mɑ:ndə] Kommandant(in); Befehlshaber(in)
favour ['feɪvə] Gefallen

Page 24

among [ə'mʌŋ] unter
*bloody ['blʌdi] blutig
to **march** [mɑ:tʃ] marschieren
to **rest** [rest] sich ausruhen
*to capture ['kæptʃə] ergreifen; einfangen
*slave [sleɪv] Sklave
dirt [dɜ:t] Schmutz; Dreck

Part 6

Page 25

*silent ['saɪlənt] still; ruhig; schweigsam; stumm
mirror ['mɪrə] Spiegel
daughter ['dɔ:tə] Tochter
thin [θɪn] dünn
*boot [bu:t] Stiefel
snow [snəʊ] Schnee

Page 26
to **steal** [sti:l] stehlen
ladyship ['leɪdiʃɪp] die gnädige Frau
maid [meɪd] Dienstmädchen
lady-in-waiting [ˌleɪdiɪn'weɪtɪŋ] Hofdame
tapestry ['tæpɪstri] Wandteppich

Page 27
scarf [skɑ:f] Schal
stall [stɔ:l] Marktstand
lord [lɔ:d] Lord; Herr
lady ['leɪdi] Lady; Dame
to **grow** [grəʊ], **grew** [gru:], **grown** [grəʊn]
hier: anbauen; züchten

Page 28
*__detective__ [dɪ'tektɪv] Detektiv/-in

Part 7
Page 29
to **spin** [spɪn] spinnen
mystery ['mɪstri] Mysterium; Rätsel; Geheimnis
quite [kwaɪt] ziemlich; ganz; völlig
*to **wake up** [weɪk‿'ʌp] aufwachen

Page 30
half an hour [ˌhɑ:f‿ən‚'aʊər] eine halbe Stunde
less [les] weniger

Part 8
Page 31
performance [pə'fɔ:məns] Aufführung

Solutions

Before you read the story

1 What was it like?

Individuelle Schülerlösungen

2 The history of Britain: Important periods

1. b, 2. e, 3. d, 4. a, 5. c

Exercises

1 Mr Marlow's shop (Part 1)

a) 1. wrong, 2. wrong, 3. wrong, 4. right, 5. right, 6. wrong
b) 1. They are all sad. 2. They can't decide what to buy. 3. They had never been in that narrow street before. 6. It's chaos.

2 Who did what in Celtic times? (Part 2)

1. both, 2. boys/men, 3. both, 4. girls/women, 5. boys/men,
6. both, 7. boys/men, 8. both, 9. girls/women, 10. both

3 Life in Celtic times (Part 2)

a) 1. rings, 2. necklaces, 3. silver, 4. gold, 5. designs, 6. tribes, 7. battles, 8. attacked, 9. care, 10. husbands', 11. generation, 12. electric, 13. fires
b) *Lösungsvorschläge:*
I <u>agree</u> with Ula that life isn't fair for girls because they have to get married early, move away from their home and take care of their husband's family. They have to cook and weave. Like the boys, they learn how to ride horses and fight with weapons, but they aren't allowed to fight in battles or have other adventures.
I <u>disagree</u> with Ula because boys have a hard life too. In the story, the boy Ula has to marry is also young and nobody asked him who he wanted to marry, so it is the same for him and for Ula. Boys and men have to work very hard so that their families have enough to eat. Also, they have to risk their lives when they fight against other tribes. A battle like that is really dangerous, not a fun adventure!

4 Imagine ... (Part 3)

Lösungsvorschläge:

a) People probably felt excited, happy or scared. They were probably excited to see new things and new people. Maybe they thought that trains were very fast and were scared that their bones would break. Or they were scared that the trains would crash.

b) *Individuelle Schülerlösungen*

5 A short summary (Part 3)

1. picks up, 2. seat, 3. Industrial Revolution, 4. factories, 5. is like, 6. blood and murder, 7. experience, 8. turn back, 9. grown up, 10. change their minds, 11. secret, 12. afford, 13. comfortable, 14. What luck

6 Back in Tudor times at the Globe Theatre (Part 4)

1. c, 2. g, 3. a, 4. d, 5. f, 6. e, 7. b

7 Good advice? (Part 4)

Lösungsvorschläge:

In 1) Olivia makes Thomas feel bad and scared that other people could be disappointed or angry at him. In 2) Olivia makes acting seem just like a little, fun thing to do. When Thomas hears this, he calms down and feels more relaxed and confident. It's much better and nicer this way.

8 Marius and Luke (Part 5)

1. C, 2. J, 3. H, 4. B, 5. I, 6. D, 7. F, 8. A, 9. E, 10. G

9 Romans in England (Page 5)

1. barracks, 2. founded, 3. emperor, 4. baths, 5. sandals, 6. weapons, 7. mood, 8. capture, 9. invaded, 10. dirt, 11. heating

Solution: Roman Empire

10 Your opinion (Part 5)

Lösungsvorschläge:

Yes, I can understand why Marius lied about his age. He wanted an adventure and he thought it would be fun to be in the Roman army with his older friends. His friends were probably proud to be in the army and Marius wanted to have fun with them. He was too young to join the army, so he *had to* lie about his age.

11 Who thinks what? (Part 6)
1. Matilda, 2. Holly, 3. Lady Beatrice, 4. Holly, 5. Matilda, 6. Linn, 7. Holly, 8. Linn, 9. Lady Beatrice, 10. Holly

12 Strange words (Part 6)
1. detective, 2. daughter, 3. snows, boots, 4. grows, 5. woke up, 6. lord, lady

13 To tell or not to tell? (Part 6)
Lösungsvorschläge:
Why Linn <u>should</u> give back the necklace:
- It's the right thing to do.
- She should feel sorry for Matilda and her family.
- She should do it because Holly asked her to.
- She should feel sorry for Lady Beatrice, who wants her necklace back.
- Her friend will probably steal more things from Lady Beatrice and more maids might get into trouble or lose their jobs.
- People could think that Linn stole the necklace herself if she sells it.

Why Linn <u>shouldn't</u> give back the necklace:
- Her family is poor too.
- Her friend will be in danger if she tells anybody that he has stolen the necklace.
- If she gives it back, Lady Beatrice might think that Linn stole the necklace herself.

14 Understanding the ending (Part 7)
Lösungsvorschläge:
a) 1. The friends have travelled to the past because they touched objects in Mr Marlow's shop. Each object is from a different historical period, so when you touch one of them, you travel back to the historical period it is from.
   2. They don't buy a present because they can't decide quickly. They want to go and eat something first, then come back and buy a present.
   3. When they go back, Mr Marlow's shop isn't there any more.

b) Mr Marlow knew that his shop would be gone when the friends come back. Maybe it's only possible to enter the shop once, and so you only have one chance to buy something.

c) *Individuelle Schülerlösungen* (Possible times/locations: Africa, Egypt, Spain, Britain during the 17th century, the early 1900s, the 1930s)

15 Five adventures, five problems (Part 8)

a) *Individuelle Schülerlösungen*

b) *Lösungsvorschlage:*

- I think Ula experiences the most difficult problem because she has to marry a boy she didn't choose herself, and she'll have to spend the rest of her life with him.
- I think Henry experiences the most difficult problem because he will have to leave the country in which he was born and will probably never be able to return. He'll never see his friends in England again.
- I think Marius experiences the most difficult problem because he's very far away from his home. Perhaps he won't be able to return. And if he tells his commander that he has lied, he could make life very difficult for Marius.
- I think Matilda experiences the most difficult problem because she could lose her job. Perhaps she won't find another job and she and her parents won't earn enough money to buy food.

Time line of British history

From around 500 BC, the **Celts** came from Europe to live in the British Isles. They lived in round houses with fires in the middle and built high walls to keep out wild animals. They had many gods.

A typical Celtic round house

500 BC

43–410 AD

After the **Romans** had arrived, the Celts moved north and west to Scotland, Ireland and Wales. The Romans built Hadrian's Wall to keep the Scots out of their part of the island of Britain.

A Roman soldier

A typical Norman castle

At the battle of Hastings, William, Duke of Normandy defeated Harold, King of the Saxons. The **Normans** ruled England for the next 88 years.

1066–1154